GREATEST FOOTBALL STARS

ACCESS THE MAGIC!

Scan the QR code to
hear this story for
FREE!

Published in the UK by Sweet Cherry Publishing Limited, 2025
Unit 36, Vulcan House, Vulcan Road,
Leicester LE5 3EF, United Kingdom

Unit 31, The Pottery, Bakers Point,
Pottery Road, Dún Laoghaire,
Dublin A96 EV18, Ireland

2 4 6 8 10 9 7 5 3 1

ISBN: 978-1-80263-542-3

Greatest Football Stars:
Bobby Moore

Text by Luke Paton
Illustrations by Sophie Jones

www.sweetcherrypublishing.com

Printed and bound in India

FSC
www.fsc.org
MIX
Paper | Supporting responsible forestry
FSC® C010615

Sweet Cherry

BOBBY MOORE

THE UNOFFICIAL STORY

WRITTEN BY
LUKE PATON

CONTENTS

1

FOOTBALL'S COMING HOME

'They think it's all over ... it is now!' screamed the commentator.

The England players slapped each other on the back, hugged and cheered. Others fell to their knees in joy, with tears of happiness rolling down their cheeks. It was a moment none of them

would ever forget.

In the 1966 World Cup, England had beaten West Germany 4-2 at Wembley Stadium!

Every England football fan had been waiting for this day since the World Cup started in 1930. The biggest prize in all of football was *finally* coming home!

Her Majesty Queen Elizabeth II clapped and smiled in the royal box. Supporters waved their Union Jack flags and filled the stadium with chants and songs. Some fans ran onto the pitch to celebrate with the team.

Each and every player in red had played their part in the historic victory. Geoff Hurst had become the first man to score a hat-trick in a World Cup final. Martin Peters had scored the second goal and challenged the Germans for 120 minutes. Gordon Banks had been strong and reliable in goal.

But the man who'd played the game of his life was their twenty-five-year-old captain: Bobby Moore.

Despite being so young, Bobby was still the calmest player on the pitch.

He went round and congratulated his teammates. 'All right. It's okay. We've done it!' he said.

Bobby then had to climb the thirty-nine steps at Wembley Stadium to accept the Jules Rimet Trophy from the queen. The Jules Rimet Trophy was awarded to World Cup winners between 1930 and 1970, and he'd be the first England captain to ever lift it!

But as he approached Her Majesty, Bobby noticed that she was wearing a beautiful gown and perfectly white gloves. He looked down at his

hands. It had been a wet day, so they were very muddy.

My God, my hands are filthy! he thought. He couldn't shake hands with the queen with dirty hands! What was he going to do?

He saw that the royal box, where the queen was waiting for him, was decorated with velvet drapes. This was his chance! Before anybody noticed, Bobby wiped some of the dirt from his hands onto the drapes.

Phew!

With slightly cleaner hands, Bobby greeted Queen Elizabeth II with a smile and accepted his winner's medal. He then took hold of the Jules Rimet Trophy and held it above his head, immediately making the crowd of 96,000 fans roar with delight.

Bobby kissed the trophy and led his squad on a lap of honour around the whole stadium.

'England! England!' the crowd cheered.

The players were national heroes!

Bobby enjoyed every second of the glory.

It was shocking to think that only a few years earlier he'd been just another footballer on the streets of Essex. The thought of playing at Wembley and winning the World Cup must have seemed like nothing more than a dream …

2

BOBBY BOY

Robert Frederick Chelsea Moore (better known as Bobby Moore) was born on the 12th of April 1941. He grew up in Barking, a town in Essex in the east of England.

Bobby started playing football in the streets outside his home with other kids. There weren't as many cars in those days, so the roads in Barking were pretty quiet. Kids could get a game going easily, only stopping occasionally to let the traffic go by.

Bobby didn't know it at the time, but those street games were an important part of his football education. He was known in later years for being a big presence in defence and standing tall, which was exactly how young Bobby had played on those concrete streets. If he fell over too much, he'd end up with very scratched knees!

It wasn't long before Bobby eventually graduated from playing in the street to playing for his school football team. He quickly became a key player in their squad and loved playing with his classmates.

Bobby's parents, Robert and Doris Moore, always encouraged him to do what he loved. They were proud of him and made sure he always looked his best on the pitch. Doris even took the time to wash and iron his bootlaces before every match!

When he was twelve years old, Bobby helped the team make it to a cup final. Unfortunately, it became Bobby's first taste of defeat ... and he didn't like it!

The team lost the game 2-1, and Bobby was absolutely heartbroken. He cried to his mother for hours! As far as he was concerned, it was the end of the world.

I want to play for England one day, he thought, *but now I can't because I'm a failure!*

Bobby's mother calmed him down. She told him it wasn't as bad as he thought, and that he had to carry on playing football if he loved it so much.

After Bobby wiped away his tears, he strapped on his boots and got back out onto the pitch.

Eventually, he moved on from the primary school in Barking to Tom Hood Grammar School in Leyton. He soon earned himself a spot on the school's football team.

But Tom Hood Grammar School was a long way from his home and Bobby hated travelling to it. He had to wake up at 7 a.m. every morning to get a bus to Barking train station, then he'd catch a train to Wanstead. After that, Bobby caught another bus to Leyton and walked to the school. By the time he got there, he was exhausted. To top it all off, some of the kids started calling him 'Tubby' because of his size! It was very horrible for Bobby. Football was the only thing that kept him going during this time.

Most wannabe players in the early 1950s idolised the England legend Stanley Matthews. His sheer talent had earned him the nicknames

'The Wizard of the Dribble' and 'The Magician'. But Bobby wasn't really interested in him. He was more impressed by club players.

Bobby was inspired by the way West Bromwich Albion's Ray Barlow played the ball calmly under pressure. He also admired Manchester United's Duncan Edwards so much that he once skipped school to watch him play against Tottenham Hotspur at White Hart Lane. Fulham's Johnny Haynes also made a big impression on young

Bobby, who admired him for his precise passing and movement.

Bobby's playing style was a combination of these qualities, and his game caught the attention of the coaches in his area. While playing for Leyton Boys, Bobby even helped the team to another cup final! His talents were so clear that clubs in the big leagues began to take notice.

One day after training with Leyton Boys, Bobby's teacher, Tom Russell, approached him. 'Bobby Moore, I'd like a word with you before you go home, please,' he said.

Bobby wasn't sure what Russell was going to say. He didn't think he'd done anything wrong ... but it turned out to be good news!

'You ought to come to West Ham to get some professional training,' Russell said. 'I'll arrange it for you and recommend you to the club.'

Bobby couldn't believe it. Of course he wanted to go and play for West Ham (nicknamed the Hammers)! His parents were happy for him to go. All he had to do now was keep playing his best football.

In 1955, West Ham manager Ted Fenton asked a scout for the club, Jack Turner, to go and watch Bobby.

Turner watched a cup match between Leyton Boys and East Ham. The final score was 3-3, and Bobby had a great game.

'Whilst he would not set the world alight, this boy certainly impressed me with his tenacity and industry,' Turner reported back to his club. This meant that Bobby had clearly shown how hardworking he was and how well he knew the game of football.

Turner's recommendation was good enough to finally get Bobby signed for West Ham. It was a major step because West Ham was in the First Division (the same level as the Premier League today).

But while Bobby was happy to sign for the club, he didn't think he had much chance of making the first team. All the other boys had played for Essex or London, and they'd at least tried out for England Schoolboys.

They have much more skill than me, Bobby thought.

But instead of letting this get him down, Bobby turned it into a positive.

If I don't have the most skill, I'm going to be more motivated than anybody else here! he thought.

However, this was the 1950s and things were very different than they are today. If a young player is signed by a team today, they do nothing more than train and play football matches. Bobby got to do these things, too – but when he signed for West Ham, he was also part of the ground staff.

If the first team had played on a

Saturday, Bobby had to help clean the Upton Park stadium on a Monday morning. He also had to get the professional players' kits ready for training and then clear them all away after practice. There were all sorts of other odd jobs as well. Bobby even had to clean the toilets from time to time!

Fridays were always the worst day for the youth team squad. If West Ham had a match on Saturday, Bobby and the other young players had to flatten the pitch by manually pushing massive rollers over it. And if that wasn't exhausting enough, they then had to clean the taps in the changing room showers. It was very hard work!

But it all paid off for Bobby. He was seventeen years old when he signed his first professional deal with West Ham. He would be paid £12 a week, which is about £350 today.

Bobby made his debut on the 8th of September 1958 against Manchester United. It was the first of 647 appearances he would make for the Hammers over the next sixteen years. He was on the way to being a club legend!

3

WEST HAM FOREVER

Bobby would be the first person to tell you he wasn't a naturally gifted footballer. He wasn't a born sprinter or an exceptional finisher. People said he couldn't play with his left foot or run very fast – but that didn't really matter. What counted was his determination.

He worked hard and listened to his coaches.

His favourite coach was West Ham's Malcolm Allison. Allison was an ex-player, and he gave Bobby two pieces of advice that he would never forget.

Allison's first piece of advice was: 'Think big.' He meant this literally, as in he wanted Bobby to stand tall on the pitch and make the opposite team think he was super strong. But Allison also wanted Bobby to think about the whole game and the whole pitch, not just his part in it. That way, he could tell people what to do and always be in the right place at the right time.

Allison's other piece of advice was beautifully simple: 'Keep forever asking yourself: If I get the ball now, who will I give it to?'

Bobby kept coming back to this advice throughout his career. Whether he was playing for West Ham or England, this question became the key to his entire game.

'If I get the ball now, who will I give it to?' he'd ask himself.

In the years to come, commentators would claim that Bobby had the best 'vision' in the world of football. He always seemed to know which player was free to pass the ball to, or which player was about to get the ball and needed to be tackled. It all came back to Allison's coaching.

Bobby was also grateful for a man named Lenny Heppell. Heppell had once been a ballroom dancer, so he didn't have any first-hand experience of football, but he still had a big impact on how Bobby played.

When Heppell first started working with West Ham's players on their balance and rhythm, Bobby wasn't too impressed.

'I can't believe in all that nonsense,' he said.

But Bobby was won over in the end. After all, Heppell had a brilliant insight into Bobby's game.

'You run as though you have a coat hanger in your shirt,' Heppell told him.

It sounds funny, but Heppell was right. Because Bobby was 'thinking big', he tended to run with a stiff upper body. This made him slow, and that was very bad when you were a defender trying to track a sprinting striker!

Heppell taught Bobby to roll his shoulders and turn with his head first instead of his body. As a result, Bobby could run faster and for longer. It was like a little magic trick!

Yet there was only so much the coaches could teach Bobby. He had to learn the rest of it out on the pitch!

After his West Ham debut against Manchester United, Bobby played in a game against Nottingham Forest.

It was Bobby's job to look after the Forest forward Johnny Quigley.

Bobby was full of confidence, as any young man would be. But Quigley soon made Bobby wish he'd spent more time in training!

Quigley ran rings around him, and Bobby wasn't prepared for the ways Quigley could easily get past him. It made him feel like a fool.

In the second half, the Forest fans in the crowd shouted, 'Play on the left half, that's the weak link!'

Bobby knew that they meant *he* was the weak link.

Nottingham Forest took advantage of his inexperience and ended up winning the game 4-0.

What am I doing here? thought Bobby after the match.

He was embarrassed to go back into the changing room. He was even more embarrassed when the newspapers were published that evening in London, all of them reminding him of how badly he'd played.

I'll never let myself get in such a state again! Bobby told himself.

He returned to the training ground more determined than ever. If he wanted to play for England one day, he had to be the best in the country!

Understandably, the West Ham manager dropped Bobby from the first team after his performance against Nottingham Forest. But Bobby slowly worked his way back into the squad. He played five times in the 1958/1959 season and thirteen times in the following season.

Then, at the age of twenty, Bobby played his first full season for West Ham. He wouldn't get dropped again for the rest of his career. Soon, Bobby would even proudly wear the captain's armband!

It was the perfect time to be a Hammers fan. West Ham was about to start competing for the first trophies in their history, with Bobby leading the way!

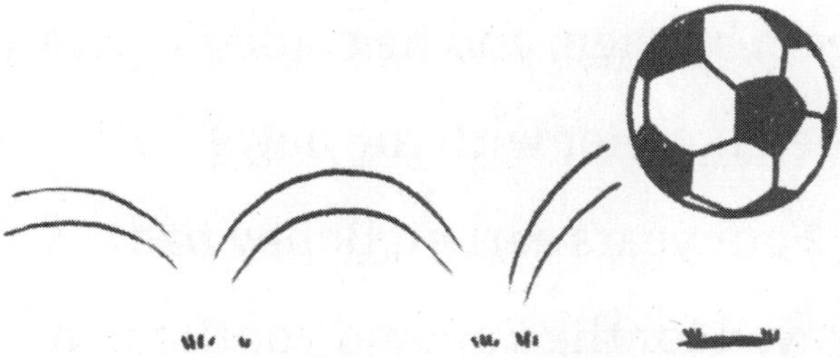

4

FA CUP MAGIC

In 1961, Ron Greenwood became the manager of West Ham. Bobby was already a regular member of the first team by then, and he couldn't have been happier with the news.

Four years earlier, Bobby had played for the England youth team

Greenwood used to manage. He remembered one of those matches as one of his best performances, giving most of the credit to Greenwood's managerial style.

With Greenwood now in charge of West Ham every week in the league, Bobby thought there was no telling just how far the team could go!

One of the reasons Greenwood had moved to West Ham was because Bobby was on the first team. He was thrilled with Bobby's potential and saw him as a key player in West Ham's future success!

Greenwood brought plenty of new ideas to the club. The first thing he did was change the formation of the team.

Back then, most clubs played in the 'WM' formation: a five-man defence and five-man attack. The defence was made up of three full-backs with two half-backs in front of them, and the attack was made up of two inside-forwards with two wingers and a centre forward in front of them.

When Greenwood joined West Ham, Bobby was playing as a half-back. Greenwood thought this was the wrong position for him.

'I want you to drop back, to play deeper and play loose,' he told Bobby during a training session in 1962.

At last, Bobby had found the ideal position for his many talents. From inside the newly-formed back four, Bobby could use his football vision and his precise tackling and passing to run the matches how he wanted.

Bobby worked very hard to make his manager proud ... but he wasn't always a fan of training. Particularly if the team were doing long-distance drills or exercises!

Whenever Greenwood demanded that his squad run for five miles through the nearby Epping Forest, they'd grumble and complain that the trek would make their calves burn. But there was no getting out of it ... unless you were as clever as Bobby!

One time, Bobby and his teammate Brian Dear managed to catch a lift on a milk float. While the others were running, the milk float drove them for most of the five miles!

'Keep up at the back, chop-chop!' Bobby joked with his teammates as he and Dear drove past, but nobody held it against them.

Bobby was so perfect for his new role in central defence that he went on to win Footballer of the Year in 1964. He was only twenty-three years old at the time – the youngest player to ever earn this incredible honour!

Part of the reason why Bobby won Footballer of the Year was because of West Ham's run in the FA Cup during the 1963/1964 season.

The team had never won the trophy before, but they successfully fought their way past Charlton Athletic,

Leyton Orient, Swindon Town, Burnley and Manchester United to set up a final against Preston North End.

About 90,000 fans filled Wembley Stadium for the occasion. The Preston supporters wore blue and white hats, while the West Ham crowd wore their famous claret and sky blue colours. The atmosphere was amazing!

The Hammers' supporters were in especially high spirits, as they expected big things from their team. West Ham was in the First Division and Preston North End was in the Second Division, so everyone assumed West Ham would easily win.

But there are no easy games in the FA Cup, especially when it comes to the final!

Preston North End started the match much stronger than West Ham. They were rewarded just ten minutes into the game when winger Doug Holden took the lead.

Goal!

West Ham weren't behind for very long. Captained by the twenty-three-year-old Bobby, the Hammers struck back almost immediately.

John Sissons teamed up with striker Johnny Byrne to score the equaliser.

It was 1-1 after only eleven minutes. The crowd didn't know what was going to happen next!

They would have to wait half an hour until the next goal ... and it was scored by Preston North End. A solid corner allowed centre-forward Alex Dawson to head the ball into the bottom corner of West Ham's net.

The players were gutted, but no one could say Preston didn't deserve to be winning at half-time. West Ham would need to play much better if they were going to turn this match around!

When the second half started, the Hammers and Bobby started playing better from the back. Seven minutes into the half, the team forced a corner.

The ball was whipped in, and Geoff Hurst got on the end of it to score.

Goal! The Hammers had made it 2-2.

There were still forty minutes left to play, and West Ham needed to use all of their experience to stop the Second Division side from scoring again.

As captain, it was Bobby's job to keep his team focussed. He played his part perfectly. He kept his defence watertight against any Preston attacks, and he swept the ball forward to the West Ham strikers as often as he could.

It took a long time, but the Hammers finally broke Preston down in the 90th minute. Midfielder Ronnie Boyce found some space in the Preston box and headed in a simple goal.

The match ended 3-2. West Ham had won the FA Cup for the first time!

Bobby led the team up those iconic thirty-nine steps of Wembley Stadium to accept the trophy. He placed his hands on the FA Cup trophy and lifted it to receive a roar from the crowd.

Bobby felt amazing. All his dreams were coming true. The FA Cup was one of the biggest prizes in English football, and he'd won it!

Little did he know that he would soon be returning to Wembley Stadium to compete in a very important competition: the European Cup Winners' Cup!

5

EUROPEAN GLORY

In 1964, everything seemed to be going Bobby's way.

He had led West Ham to FA Cup victory, been voted Footballer of the Year *and* captained the international England football team for the very first time. All this, and he was still only twenty-three years old!

He had good news at home, too. He and his wife, Tina, were going to have a baby!

But Bobby still wasn't fully happy. Throughout the second half of 1964, he was actually in quite a lot of pain. There was an almost unbearable discomfort in his groin, so he went to see the West Ham physio about it.

'A training injury,' the physio said. 'It will wear off.'

Bobby did his best to ignore it and

carry on playing football. But the pain never went away.

One day, Tina rolled over in bed and accidentally knocked into Bobby. He shot awake with a scream of agony.

'You can't ignore it any longer,' Tina urged him. 'You have to see a doctor. You have to know.'

Bobby knew she was right and immediately took her advice.

The doctors quickly diagnosed him with testicular cancer. This was a life-threatening illness, and Bobby needed surgery if he was going to survive it. He scheduled the operation for as soon as possible.

'Don't tell anyone what I'm in here for,' Bobby said to Tina, after he went in for the surgery.

The illness was nothing to be embarrassed about, but Bobby wanted it to be kept a secret. Bobby lived in different times, and he was worried people wouldn't be very understanding about it.

Besides, he was always a quiet and private man, so he didn't think anybody would ask any questions.

After the operation, Bobby had to take time away from football to recover. But amazingly, he was only out of the Hammers' lineup for three months!

What a man, thought Tina, who was very proud of her husband.

On the 24th of January 1965, while Bobby was in recovery, Tina gave birth to their daughter Roberta.

Soon enough, Bobby was back on the pitch doing what he did best!

He even helped West Ham go on a spectacular run in the European Cup Winners' Cup.

The competition was a highly respected knock-out tournament featuring clubs from all over Europe. If a team won a domestic cup one season, they would be able to compete for the European Cup Winners' Cup the next season. So, because West Ham had won the FA Cup in 1964, they played in the European Cup Winners' Cup in 1965.

It was far from an easy tournament. West Ham had to beat La Gantoise from Belgium, Sparta Prague from Czechoslovakia and Lausanne Sport from Switzerland just to get to the semi-final.

Their semi-final opponents were Real Zaragoza from Spain. This would be a real challenge for the Hammers. Zaragoza's forwards – Marcelino, Canário, Carlos Lapetra, Eleuterio Santos and Juan Manuel Villa – were so famous that they even had a special name: the Magnificent Five!

But Bobby was not afraid of anybody, and he always performed his best on the biggest occasions. He held his defence strong against the Zaragoza attacking force, guiding his team to a historic 3-2 victory over two legs.

On the 9th of May 1965, West Ham faced 1860 Munich in the final of the European Cup Winners' Cup.

'Here's our chance to show the world what we can do,' manager Ron Greenwood told his team before the match.

Bobby took those words to heart and pushed his team to play their finest football yet.

The match was full of end-to-end football. The commentators said it was 'magnificent' and full of 'bold and imaginative' play. They hailed it as a 'triumph for West Ham and a triumph for the game of football.' Many of the West Ham fans who filled Wembley Stadium agreed that it was the best they'd ever seen their team play.

Bobby and Greenwood also thought it was the best *Bobby* had ever played, too. The match was made even sweeter because the team won 2-0!

Bobby even played a part in West Ham's second goal! It was his pinpoint cross that eventually found its way to forward Alan Sealey, who then scored.

For the second time in twelve months, Bobby climbed Wembley's thirty-nine steps to the royal box to claim a trophy West Ham had never won before. It was magic!

Bobby realised he'd played in two finals at Wembley Stadium. The first time he'd won a domestic cup, and the second time he'd won a European cup. Now all he needed to complete the set was an international cup ...

6

ROAD TO VICTORY

Bobby had debuted for England's first team back in 1962. He'd received the news of his call-up from Ron Greenwood. At the time, Greenwood was Bobby's manager at both West Ham and the England under 23s team. When Bobby was asked to go to

Greenwood's office, he thought they'd be talking about the U23 side's upcoming games in Rhodesia and Nigeria. But he was wrong.

'You won't be coming with us on the trip,' Greenwood told Bobby.

Bobby was shocked and angry. 'Why?' he demanded. 'What have I done wrong?'

Bobby knew he'd been playing well for club and country. There was no reason why he should be dropped!

Then Greenwood smiled. 'Walter wants you to go with him to Chile,' he said.

Bobby didn't understand at first … then it slowly dawned on him. Walter Winterbottom was the manager of the England first team, and England was about to play in the 1962 World Cup in Chile.

Bobby was going to be a member of a World Cup England squad!

It was an incredible experience for Bobby. He played in every game, and his performances confirmed his position in the England first team. England were unfortunately knocked out of the competition in the quarter-final by the eventual winners, Brazil.

It was a sad blow for the England team, and Winterbottom resigned as manager not long after they returned home from Chile. But it was only the beginning of Bobby's international career!

In 1963, Alf Ramsey took over as manager of England and almost immediately gave Bobby the captain's armband. Bobby couldn't believe it. He was only twenty-two years old at the time! He was the youngest England captain ever!

His first game in charge of the team came on the 29th of May 1963. The match was against Czechoslovakia, and it proved to be the perfect show of Bobby's leadership skills. His England team beat Czechoslovakia 4-2!

Bobby wasn't the kind of captain who shouted at his players or threw things at them. He was upright and serious on the pitch, and he commanded his team with respect. But he also made great friends in the squad and knew how to have some fun off the field.

One of Bobby's favourite things to do was to call his players by the wrong names. At the start of some England games, Bobby would have to introduce the team to an important person from the country they were playing in. To have a bit of fun, Bobby would tell them Jimmy Greaves was Roger Hunt, or Ray Wilson was George Cohen. The official wouldn't have any idea what was happening, and the players got to have a laugh!

Another time, the England team were playing in New York City when Bobby told his roommate, Jimmy Greaves, that they were going out.

'Where we going?' asked Greaves.

'I want to see Ella Fitzgerald,' replied Bobby.

Even though the manager had told the players not to stay out late, Bobby did it anyway. He and Greaves snuck out of their rooms and got to see the singer Ella Fitzgerald perform. But they also got in a bit of trouble with the manager!

Luckily, none of this made a difference to Bobby's football. By 1966, he was ready to lead England to World Cup glory!

England had been chosen to host the tournament, which made it even more special and exciting. The country couldn't wait to see how their team performed on the world stage.

However, England's 1966 World Cup campaign didn't get off to a good start – to put it mildly! Their first game was against Uruguay, and it ended in a 0-0 draw. This was the first time a team hosting the World Cup hadn't won their opening match.

Football pundit Jimmy Hill expressed the nation's disappointment when he said on TV, 'England will not win the World Cup, but don't blame the manager. No one could win with these players.'

But Ramsey had promised England a World Cup victory, and he wasn't going to give up without a fight!

Ramsey told his players, 'Gentlemen, we are building a team, a real team, and what matters now is how we progress in this tournament.

Rest assured, we will win and have the satisfaction and pride of it for the rest of our lives.'

The motivational team talk worked. England went on to beat Mexico 2-0 and France 2-0, finishing at the top of their group. This meant they would advance to the knock-out stages of the tournament. More importantly for Bobby, it meant nobody had scored against England for the whole competition.

There wasn't a round of 16 stages in the World Cup back then, so the team went straight to the quarter-final.

Their opponents were Argentina. It was going to be a very different game from the others they'd played. The Argentinians were much more physical than other teams, and they would try to muscle the English players off the ball.

'Well, gentleman,' said Ramsey before the game, 'you know the sort of game you have on your hands this afternoon.'

The match was a bruising contest. The Argentinian player Antonio Rattin was sent off, and he got so mad that it took some police officers to finally get him off the pitch!

It was a difficult game, but Bobby and England did their best to stay calm. The team finally triumphed 1-0!

They would face Portugal next in the semi-final.

Portugal had a striker called Eusébio, who many people considered to be one of the best players in the world. Some people thought he was even better than Pelé!

Bobby and his England team were going to have to keep a close watch on him – and that's exactly what they did.

Eusébio did manage to score the first goal of the competition against England, but Bobby Charlton scored two at the other end.

'Well done, gentlemen,' Ramsey said after the 2-1 victory. 'You have just earned your chance.'

England were going to the World Cup final!

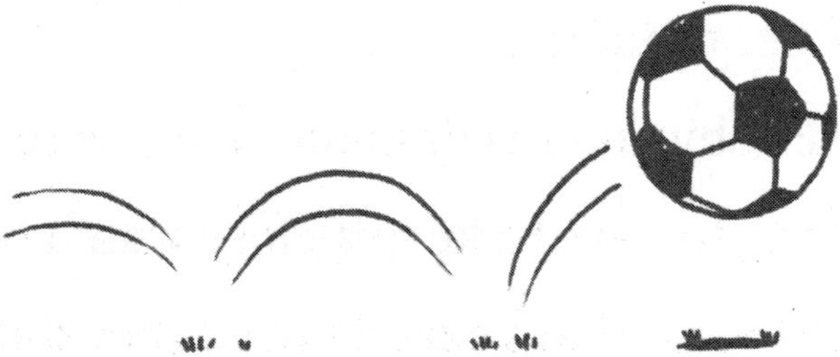

7

WORLD CUP FINAL

On the 30th of July 1966, the World Cup final took place at Wembley Stadium. It was truly a day to remember.

Fans filled the stands way before the teams even made it out onto the pitch. They sang and cheered and revelled in the incredible atmosphere.

When the Royal Marines' band played the national anthem ahead of the match, it seemed like everybody sang *God Save the Queen* at the top of their voices!

The support wasn't lost on the players, who were nervously waiting in the changing rooms before kick-off.

'This is the most important game of my life,' said Bobby.

He believed England had a team capable of winning the World Cup – all they had to do now was prove it.

Their opponents that day were West Germany – a very good side. While England had only managed a 0-0 draw with Uruguay, West Germany had beaten them 4-0 in the quarter-final.

'You're better than them,' Ramsey told his team before the match. 'You can beat them. But never forget they're not beaten until the final whistle goes and you're one goal in front.'

As the team's captain, Bobby led his players out onto the field. Then he stood on the centre spot opposite the German captain, Uwe Seeler.

They shook hands, exchanged flags and then got down to business.

Bobby won the coin toss and chose for West Germany to begin kick-off.

If anybody had been expecting a nervy or hesitant start, they were in for a shock. It only took eleven minutes for West Germany to open the scoring.

Bobby was devastated. He was close to charging down the shot from Helmut Haller, but it slipped under his legs and somehow found its way past goalkeeper Gordon Banks. It was the first goal any team had scored against England in open play during that World Cup!

But Bobby still believed in his team. He knew they could get back into the game!

Seven minutes later, Bobby was fouled by Wolfgang Overath and awarded a free kick. Bobby immediately got the ball and looked up.

In the box, his West Ham teammate Geoff Hurst was making a run towards goal. Bobby took the free kick quickly, flighting it perfectly onto Hurst's head and ...

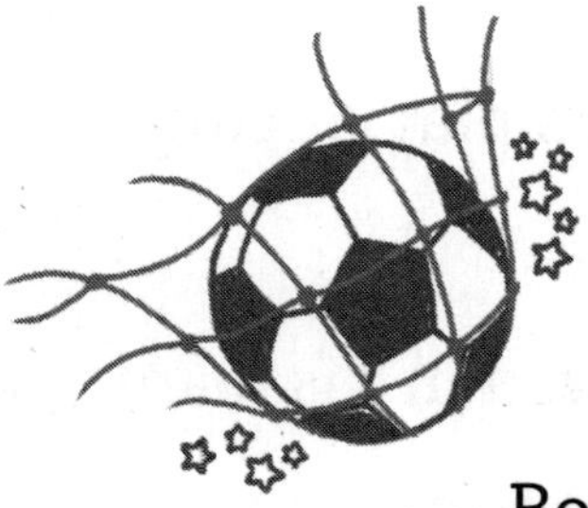

Goal!

'A brilliant piece of football there by Bobby Moore,' exclaimed the TV commentator.

Although England had levelled the score, there was plenty of work left to do. But at least now they had some momentum.

The score stayed the same through to half-time and into the second half.

The crowd did their best to cheer on the team. 'When the reds go marching in!' they chanted, referring to England's red shirts.

In the 78th minute, England finally broke the deadlock.

Hurst tried a shot, but it was deflected by a West Germany defender. Luckily, the ball landed perfectly for Martin Peters (another West Ham player) to blast it home!

It was 2-1 to England!

There were only thirteen minutes left to play, and Bobby felt certain they were going to win the match. He could hear the crowd roaring, 'We want three! We want three!' They were happy, and Bobby was happy too. The game was almost over.

Then disaster struck!

In the very last minute of play, Wolfgang Weber scored an equaliser from close range.

'How did you let that happen?' Bobby asked his defence.

They were so close to victory and now they'd have to play extra time! That meant another thirty minutes of anxious football.

Bobby knew they only had themselves to blame. They'd sealed the game up, only to let victory slip away from them at the last moment.

It was going to take every bit of strength they had to pick themselves up and try again.

Ramsey gathered the team around for a team talk. He pointed out that the West Germany team were noticeably even more exhausted than England. Their last-ditch effort to score the equaliser had taken a lot of energy out of them.

'You've won it once,' Ramsey told his men. 'Now you must win it again.'

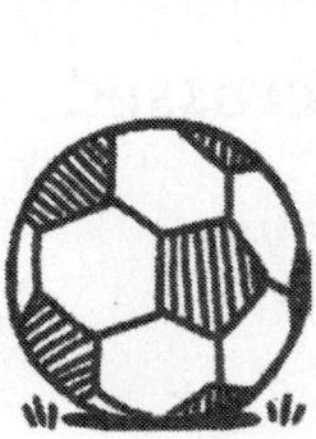

We have to pull out everything we have! Bobby thought.

Ten minutes into extra time, Hurst fired a shot that clattered the crossbar and then bounced over the line ... Or did it?

The England players celebrated as if they had scored, but West Germany's players complained that the ball had bounced *on* the line – not *over* it. The referee asked his assistant whether the ball had crossed the line. The assistant said it *had* crossed the line, and the goal was given.

England were 3-2 up!

The West Germany players were annoyed that the referees had given the goal, but the England side were thrilled – as were the crowd.

'We want four! We want four!' they began to chant.

Bobby gave them what they wanted in the last minute of extra time.

West Germany threw everything they had at the English defence in the dying minutes of the match. England either had to stay alert or finish the game off with another goal.

When the ball fell to Bobby in the 120th minute, he looked up and made a very important decision. Instead of kicking it out of play, he saw Hurst in acres of space and clipped the ball towards him. Hurst picked it up ... and smashed the ball into the top of West Germany's net!

The game was over at 4-2 to England!

England's fans ran onto the pitch to celebrate with the players, the crowds began to sing, chant and cheer – and they even screamed for the manager. 'Ramsey, Ramsey!' they called.

Some players even fell to the ground in relief, while others celebrated by dancing. No one knew quite what to do or how to react!

Bobby stayed calm on the outside, but he was buzzing on the inside. They'd done what no English team had done before and made history.

Then, for the third year in a row, Bobby climbed the infamous thirty-nine steps at Wembley Stadium to accept their trophy. Fans clapped him on the back as he made his way back down onto the pitch, clutching the Jules Rimet Trophy.

Bobby kept hold of the World Cup trophy for as long as he could. At one point, he even dared to throw it up into the air and catch it. The crowd loved it.

'Ee-aye-addio, we've won the Cup!' they sang.

Fans followed the team from the pitch to the hotel where the players would enjoy a marvellous banquet to celebrate. Bobby waved and cheered along with them.

'England! England!' they chanted.

'On behalf of all the lads, I would

like to say our supporters have been marvellous,' Bobby said. 'It was a wonderful performance.'

The party showed no sign of ending in the weeks after their World Cup victory. Bobby and West Ham even took the Jules Rimet Trophy to matches with them to show the fans!

Bobby had more reasons to celebrate than most. He was named as part of the All-Star Team of the World Cup, and he was also named as the Player of the Tournament!

For his extraordinary achievement, Bobby later received the BBC Sports

Personality of the Year award and an OBE from the queen.

'Well done on winning the World Cup,' the queen told Bobby when he accepted his OBE. 'I saw the game, and I enjoyed it very much. It was wonderful for us.'

'Thank you very much indeed,' said Bobby. He made sure he had clean hands when he got his OBE, too!

But Ramsey would later give Bobby the biggest compliment of all.

'If people say England would not have won the World Cup without me as manager, I can say it would have been impossible without Bobby Moore as captain,' he said. 'He was the heartbeat of the team in 1966. He was my right-hand man, my lieutenant on the field, a cool calculated footballer I could trust with my life.'

8
THE MISSING BRACELET

Bobby became one of the most famous and beloved footballers in England after the team's historic World Cup win. He was proud to remain the captain of England after 1966, of course, but his life also got better away from the pitch.

In 1965, Bobby and Tina welcomed a son, Dean, into the family. And thanks to Bobby's newfound fame and success, he could provide a better life for his growing family. It meant he could bring happiness to other people, too.

Bobby didn't like to make a fuss about it, but he also enjoyed working with the Thalidomide Trust – a charity that helps people living with disabilities.

On one occasion, Bobby spent the day with children born without limbs who were supported by the

Thalidomide Trust. He played football with them and asked about their favourite football teams.

'Who do you support?' Bobby asked one boy.

'West Ham,' said the boy. 'Who do you support?'

Bobby smiled. 'Who do you think I support? My wife and kids!' he joked.

Everybody was happy for him, but there was one thing that would make football fans even happier. They

wanted to see him lead the England football team to even more success!

By that point, England was one of the best teams in the world under Bobby's guidance. They were real contenders to win the World Cup trophy again in the next tournament in 1970.

But before Bobby could play the first game of the 1970 World Cup, the strangest event of his entire life took place. And it had nothing to do with football. It was all about a missing bracelet.

Ahead of the 1970 World Cup in Mexico, England were preparing to play a pre-tournament round of warm up matches. The first team they had to face was Colombia, so they were staying in a hotel in the capital city of Bogotá.

While waiting for their hotel rooms to be ready, Bobby and his friend and teammate Bobby Charlton went to the hotel jewellery shop called Fuego Verde. Charlton thought he might be able to find a nice ring to take home to his wife. He asked the shop assistant about a ring, and they talked about the price. In the end, he decided that it was too expensive.

The two footballers left the shop without buying anything and went back to the hotel foyer. They expected it would be the last time they ever thought about the Fuego Verde shop.

How wrong they were.

Moments later, the Fuego Verde shop assistant came out and pointed at them.

Bobby had no idea what was going on, but things started to get worse very quickly. The police got involved, and both players were pulled aside for questioning.

The shop assistant claimed that a very expensive bracelet had gone missing from the shop … and that *Bobby Moore* had stolen it!

Bobby was very honest with the police. He hadn't stolen the bracelet, so he had nothing to hide! The police eventually seemed satisfied that everything was in order and it all went quiet.

Bobby tried to forget about the bracelet as the England team played in a 0-4 thrashing of Colombia the next day, and again when they beat Ecuador 0-2 in Ecuador.

But the story of the bracelet kept getting weirder.

The England team had to stop in Bogotá again before they headed to Mexico to start their World Cup campaign. Bobby thought he was only supposed to be in Bogotá for a few hours, but he ended up staying for four days!

In Bogotá, the police wanted to keep Bobby in a jail cell to answer more questions about the supposed theft of the bracelet. Bobby was very relieved when the judge agreed that he could stay under house arrest with the Colombian FA President instead.

Worryingly, the Fuego Verde shop assistant was still saying that Bobby was guilty of stealing the bracelet. She was sure that nobody else had taken it.

Other witnesses in the case against Bobby weren't as consistent with their stories. One man claimed he'd seen Bobby slip the bracelet into the pocket of his tracksuit. The problem was, Bobby didn't have a pocket in his tracksuit!

Colombian officials were soon forced to admit that the case against Bobby didn't hold up, and Bobby was set free.

'I am happy the allegations against me turned out to be groundless,' Bobby said in a statement to the press. The Colombian chief of police later revealed he thought the whole thing was a scam designed to get money out of the England captain.

All Bobby really wanted to do was get on with the business of playing football. This strange case of the missing bracelet was a major distraction from the fact that England had a World Cup title to defend!

Everything's going to be fine when we start preparing for the World Cup once again, thought Bobby.

Thankfully, he was right.

Despite all the drama in Bogotá, Bobby still captained the England team in Mexico. He played well in their first game of the tournament, and the team beat Romania 1-0.

The next match was an interesting tie against Brazil. For many fans watching at home, the game was the main event of the group stage during the 1970 World Cup.

Brazil had already won the World Cup twice, and they were the favourite to take home the trophy once again. The star of their squad was Pelé – arguably one of the greatest forwards to ever play the game.

Bobby loved getting the opportunity to play against Pelé. After all, if he wanted to be the greatest defender in footballing history, he had to play against the very best strikers.

The match certainly didn't disappoint. Two moments in the game are still talked about today as some of the best plays in football.

In the first half, Brazil's Jairzinho drove towards the byline and crossed the ball back to Pelé. Pelé leapt into the air, headed the ball towards goal and waited for it to find the back of the net. Everybody was sure it was going to be a goal!

Everybody except England's goalkeeper, Gordon Banks.

His incredible acrobatic save pushed the ball out for a corner instead. Bobby immediately congratulated Banks with a mighty smack on his behind! It was the greatest save anybody had ever seen.

But the best moment in the game belonged to Bobby.

Bobby made many tackles in that match, with most fans agreeing it was his best ever display in an England shirt. But the tackle everybody talked about saw him shadowing Jairzinho into the box. If he timed his challenge even half a second wrong, Brazil would have been awarded a penalty. But Bobby nipped the ball off the Brazilian's toes at exactly the right moment, confirming that he was definitely one of England's all-time greats.

Despite their efforts, Bobby and England couldn't keep Brazil out forever. Jairzinho's goal for Brazil in the 60th minute was enough to triumph, and the match ended 1-0.

At the end of the match, Bobby and Pelé exchanged smiles, respect and shirts.

'See you in the final,' said Bobby.

'I think you will,' said Pelé.

Bobby did his best to cheer up the team in the changing rooms afterwards. 'Come on,' he said. 'We may have lost, but we're still in this!'

But Bobby's prediction didn't come true. England was knocked out in the quarter-final stage by their old foes, West Germany.

Bobby didn't know it at the time, but that match against West Germany was the last World Cup game he would ever play.

9

RECORD BREAKER

Bobby still had plenty of football left to play after the 1970 World Cup. Before he chose to retire in 1978, Bobby smashed records for the number of appearances for both West Ham and England.

His final game for England came

in 1973 in a friendly against Italy. It was Bobby's 108th cap, but it was hardly a game to celebrate. The Italians won 1-0.

While he was playing that match, Bobby knew it was his last game for England. Nobody made an announcement and nobody said anything in the changing rooms. But England had failed to qualify for the World Cup in 1974, and Bobby was smart enough to realise what that meant.

'The next World Cup is four years away,' he said. 'It's time for younger guys, fresh faces. I know they don't need old Mooro anymore.'

Bobby captained the Three Lions for ninety of his 108 international matches, and the team only lost thirteen times under his leadership. At the time of his retirement, Bobby held the record for most England caps for an outfield player. This record lasted until 2009, when David Beckham finally broke it.

Bobby achieved a similar feat for West Ham in the same year. He made

his 509th appearance for his club in 1973, smashing the previous record. But Bobby didn't stop there. By the time Bobby left West Ham in 1974, he'd made a whopping 647 appearances for the Hammers. Since then, only two other men have played for West Ham more times than Bobby!

There was a reason Bobby stopped at 647 games. He'd spent sixteen years with West Ham and thought it was time for a change.

Bobby decided to transfer to Fulham.

He knew some players who'd enjoyed their time at the club, and he already had friends in the squad.

The Fulham fans were ecstatic that the golden boy of English football had come to their club. For Bobby's first game, 18,000 supporters (twice as many as usual) turned up to see him play.

Unfortunately for Bobby, the match was against Middlesborough. Their team were in good form that season, and Fulham found themselves 0-4 down within the first twenty minutes of Bobby's debut.

Bobby put an arm around his friend and teammate Alan Mullery. 'I think I might have made a mistake, mate,' he joked.

It wasn't all bad at Fulham, though. In the 1974/1975 season, Bobby helped them reach the FA Cup final. It was a bittersweet moment for Bobby. On the one hand, he would be making another visit to Wembley. On the other, it would be the last chance he'd get to play on that famous turf.

West Ham ended up winning the game 2-0, but Bobby couldn't be sad about the result.

He approached Mullery after the final whistle. 'Did you enjoy it?' he asked his teammate.

'No, I didn't really, because we got beat!' Mullery said. He was feeling a bit down in the dumps.

'Hold on!' said Bobby. 'Two guys our age shouldn't be playing in cup finals. We should have enjoyed it!'

Bobby stayed with Fulham until 1977. He played his 1,000th first team match with them. Then he rounded off his career in a move that has since been copied by the likes of David Beckham and Lionel Messi: he moved to North America. Bobby played for San Antonio Thunder and then Seattle Sounders.

Bobby was still loved by sports fans all over the world, and there was no way he was going to completely leave football behind when he finally retired. The only question was, what would he do next?

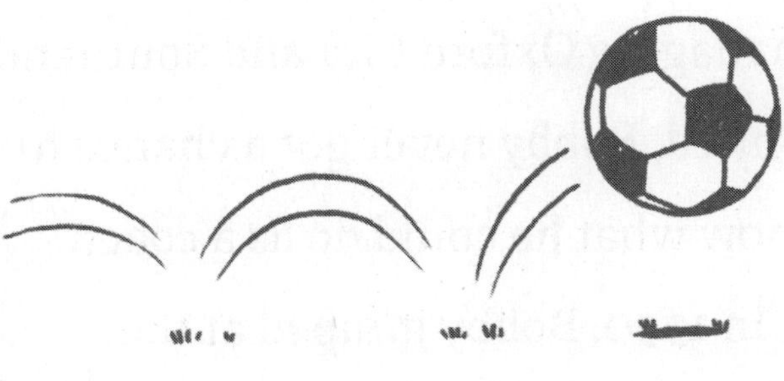

10

A LASTING LEGACY

Like many players, Bobby wanted to be a football manager after he hung up his boots. But after short attempts managing Oxford City and Southend United, Bobby never got a chance to show what he could do as a coach.

In 1990, Bobby jumped at the

chance to be a match analyst for the radio station Capital Gold. The job meant he could be part of football without the pressure of managing a team.

His co-commentator during this period was Jonathan Pearce, and the two of them became great friends. Bobby would drive them both to matches all over England. 'You do all the real work, Pearco, and need to be fresh,' Bobby said.

Everybody wanted to know what Bobby thought of the games.

'What did Bobby say about me in the commentary?' the players would ask. 'What did Bobby think about me?'

The job fed Bobby's passion for the game. He picked out Rio Ferdinand as a future star when he was just a young boy at West Ham.

And when England lost in the semi-finals of the 1990 World Cup on penalties, Bobby cried his eyes out.

The following year, there was good news in Bobby's personal life. After his marriage to Tina ended in 1986, Bobby eventually met somebody new.

Her name was Stephanie, and they got married in December 1991.

Then something exciting also happened in Bobby's professional life: he and Jonathan Pearce won a Sony Radio Academy Award!

Sadly, his promising commentary career was cut tragically short.

The last game Bobby commentated on was a 6-0 England victory over San Marino at Wembley. 'They got the job done in the end,' Bobby said. 'You can't complain when you win 6-0.'

Bobby did a good job commentating on the game, but everybody knew he was in pain. The night before the match, Bobby had announced to the world that he was suffering from bowel cancer.

He was due to return to Upton Park later that week to commentate on a West Ham game, but Pearce had convinced him to stay at home.

Sadly, Bobby died on the 24th of February 1993. He was only fifty-one years old.

After Bobby's death, the tributes came flooding

in from all the people who knew and loved him.

Pelé said, 'Of all the defenders I have challenged, Bobby Moore was the fairest, the best and the most honourable.'

West Germany footballer Franz Beckenbauer said Bobby was the 'best defender in the history of the game.'

Scottish manager Jock Stein said, 'There should be a law against him. He knows what's happening twenty minutes before everyone else.'

Bobby later became the first player in the English Football Hall of Fame.

He was named as one of the BBC's 100 Greatest Britons, and UEFA labelled him the 'Golden Player of England'. Bobby also became the very first footballer to get an English Heritage Blue Plaque, which was placed outside his childhood home in Barking.

Two weeks after Bobby died, West Ham held an emotional ceremony in honour of the greatest player to step foot in Upton Park. Former Hammers players and World Cup winners Geoff Hurst and Martin Peters spread a number 6 shirt made of flowers on the centre spot. The Hammers retired Bobby's famous number 6 shirt in 2008 to mark fifty years since Bobby had made his Upton Park debut.

West Ham also named a stand at Upton Park after Bobby, and in 2016 the Bobby Moore Stand moved with the team to their new home at the London Stadium. The most touching tributes from his former club were two statues. One shows Bobby Moore, Geoff Hurst, Martin Peters and Ray

Wilson celebrating after their 1966 World Cup victory. The other shows the players celebrating their 1965 European Cup Winners' Cup glory.

Bobby's brilliance on the football field has been memorialised in other more amusing ways as well. In the famous *Three Lions* song, there's the lyric, 'I still see that tackle by Moore.' This is a reference to Bobby's famous tackle on Jairzinho in the 1970 World Cup!

There was also the time an airline used an image of Bobby on the tail fin of one of its massive aeroplanes. And best of all, Bobby became a playable character in a popular video game series. Fans finally got to know what it was like to play with Bobby!

But Bobby would probably be most proud of the legacy he left behind *off* the pitch.

After Bobby's death, his second wife, Stephanie, set up the Bobby Moore Fund for Cancer Research UK. The goal was to raise money and awareness to help people suffering from bowel cancer – the disease that eventually ended Bobby's life. In the three decades since Bobby passed away, the Bobby Moore Fund has raised more than £30 million for Cancer Research.

Bobby's daughter, Roberta, also created the Moore Family Foundation in 2014 in memory of Bobby.

'My family are incredibly excited about the creation of this project, which we hope will make a real difference to lives of young people in the area of the country Bobby loved more than any other,' she said.

In 2005, the FA asked football fans to choose who they thought was the greatest England player of the past fifty years. Unsurprisingly, Bobby easily won the poll!

Sculptor Philip Jackson then spent two years creating a six-metre-tall statue of Bobby to take pride of place in front of the new Wembley Stadium. The sculptor wanted a monument that showed off Bobby's honesty, loyalty, leadership, popularity and humble nature.

'He was one of the greatest footballers the world has ever seen,' said Bobby Charlton, as he unveiled the statue to the public. 'He was captain in 1966. England had the perfect leader. Had it not been for him we probably would not have won the World Cup.'

This last tribute to Bobby has been seen by millions of football fans all over the world. Now every time they walk down Olympic Way towards Wembley Stadium to support the Three Lions or the Lionesses, Bobby watches over them.

Bobby would've been proud of the fans choosing him for the statue, and no doubt would've been impressed with the finished sculpture. But he might have been slightly embarrassed with the gushing inscription written beneath it ... even though it is a perfect memorial for this national hero.

It says: *Immaculate footballer. Imperial defender. Immortal hero of 1966. First Englishman to raise the World Cup aloft. Favourite son of London's East End.*

Finest legend of West Ham United.

National Treasure. Master of Wembley.

Lord of the game. Captain extraordinary.

Gentleman of all time.